MW00528691

ESSAY PRESS

Y AN ESSAY

The Body: An Essay was first published by Slope Editions in the spring of 2002.

Before it was published in book form, sections of The Body first appeared in Another Chicago Magazine, Both, Conduit, Seneca Review, and VeRT. Excerpts have been anthologized in The Best American Poetry 2002, The Next American Essay, and Contemporary Voices from the East: A Norton Anthology.

Author's note from the first edition: I wish to thank the following persons who made offerings of support, advice, inspiration, and more: John D'Agata, E., Robert Kelly, John Matthias, and Tristram. I remain, as ever, theirs, &c.

Author's note to the current edition: For love during the long-haul and always and evermore, I dedicate this book to Catherine, Pea-Gay, my mother and father, and Honey Bear.

1. It was the particular feel of him that made me want to go back: everything that is said is said underneath, where, if it does matter, to acknowledge it is to let on to your embarrassment. That I love you makes me want to run and hide.

2. It is not the story I know or the story you tell me that matters; it is what I already know, what I don't want to hear you say. Let it exist this way, concealed; let me always be embarrassed, knowing that you know that I know but pretend not to know.

3. One thing the great poet confessed before biting into her doughnut: a good poem writes itself as if it doesn't care — never let on that within this finite space, your whole being is heavy with a need to emote infinitely.

4. I never uttered that loose word; I only said, "I opened my legs and let him."

5. One thing the great poet would never confess was that afterwards, she took me into the back room and slapped me for loving her.

6. The visit to the circus is of particular import if one considers this passage from a letter written to the man whom she regarded as her guardian angel (to whom she also dedicated a great number of poems). Dated in her 23rd year, the letter states:

... I told Lousine that I was terrified of clowns; no, not just childishly afraid like being afraid of the dark, but really, really fearful, like starting-your-period-for-the-first-time scared. Anyhow, she looked at me serious-like and made me promise in that strong Armenian-Brooklyn way of hers that I would never reveal this to anyone because anyone could be an enemy. She made me swear up and down and on graves and holy books and the needle in the eye and all sorts of crazy shit that drove me insane. I can't help but think now that something bad is waiting to happen and that there's this little man staring at me from between the fence slats. I can see his little eyeball sometimes, showing up in the various holes in my apartment. But you know what scares me the most? It's that clown in *Anthony and Cleopatra* who says to Cleopatra, "You must not think I am so simple but I know the devil himself will not eat a woman. I know that a woman is a dish for the gods, if the devil dress her not. But truly, these same whoreson devils do the gods great harm in their women; for in every ten that they make, the devils mar five." So you see, Andy, I have been seriously stressed. Am I marred? E. says he cannot love me now and that I have a dark side he is afraid of ...

7. It wasn't that the ice-cream man came everyday; he came whenever the child heard his music.

8. The confessions denoted here are lies, as it would be senseless to list my true regrets. The true regrets are indexed under the subject heading "BUT EVERYONE DIES LIKE THIS," found at the end of the text.

9. Given this information, the definition of "footnote" is of particular interest to the overall understanding of "bedlam." Consider, for instance, this denotation: *n.2. Something related to but of lesser importance than a larger work or occurrence.*

10. See also De Sica's *Bicycle Thief*; thus the leitmotif of this body: *What will I have found in the end if I am seeking as if I am seeking one thing in particular?*

11. The great pre-Socratic philosopher Empedocles did not keep the commentative sound of his life a secret. He says of the source of mortal things, one should "know these things distinctly, having heard the story from a god" (As told by Simplicus, *Commentary on Aristotle's Physics* 160.1-1 = 31B23).

12. It should be understood that Heraclitus also lost a bicycle. In *Miscellanies* (2.17.4 = 22B18), Clement of Alexandria quotes Heraclitus as saying, "Unless he hopes for the unhoped for, he will not find it, since it is not to be hunted out and is impassable."

13. *I Corinthians* 13:5 "Doth not behave itself unseemly, seeketh not her own, is not easily provoked, thinketh no evil"; 13:7 "Beareth all things, believeth all things, hopeth all things, endureth all things"; 13:11 "When I was a child, I spake as a child, I understood as a child, I thought as a child: but when I became a woman, I put away childish things"; 13:12 "For now we see through a glass, darkly; but then face to face: now I know in part; but then shall I know even as also I am known." Given these passages, it is easy for the reader to infer that the protagonist, aside from despising her pubic hair, also believed that she was being watched and thus began her odd behavior of hiding and casting her voice into a void.

14. Ms. Boully must have been confused, as it was actually _____, not _____, who uttered "_____"
and thus became such a symbolic figure in her youth; however, critic and playwright Lucia Del Vecchio (who is known to transcribe some of her dialogue directly from audiocassettes she and Boully recorded during their undergraduate years), argues that Boully was well acquainted with _____.
As this is a suspicious oversight, Del Vecchio cites evidence from a recorded conversation where Boully argues _____.

15. Although the text implies a great flood here, know this is seen through a child's eyes, and here she actually played in sprinklers while loving Heraclitus: "A lifetime [or eternity] is a child playing, playing checkers; the kingdom belongs to a child" (Hippolytus, *Refutation* 9.9.4 = 22B52).

16. The circus net, under the trapeze artists and tightrope walkers, is to be interpreted as "a safe way to know falling."

17. Although the narrative is rich with detail and historical accounts, the author is blatantly supplying false information. For example, the peaches were not rotten and there were no flies or rain for that matter. The man she claims to have kissed never existed, or rather, the man existed; however, she never kissed him, and because she never kissed him, she could only go on living by deluding herself into believing that he never existed.

18. The last time I saw the great poet I brought her strawberries, hoping she would ask me to bed. Instead, she only suggested that I touch how soft her fuzzy pink sweater was. I broke down crying as soon as I made my confession. I told her that I had written a bad poem, that in the space between me and him, I emoted too much through speech and touch, and I made it known that I was willing to emote infinitely; the poem was so bad, he left. I was hoping that the great poet would kiss me then, but instead, she slapped me and forbade me from telling anyone that I was her student. I left her, and I never told her that I was on my hands and knees, picking those berries for her.

19. Cf. Delmore Schwartz:

> Disturb me, compel me. It is not true
> That "no man is happy," but that is not
> The sense which guides you. If we are
> Unfinished (we are, unless hope is a bad dream),
> You are exact. You tug my sleeve
> Before I speak, with a shadow's friendship,
> And I remember that we who move
> Are moved by clouds that darken midnight.

20. Obviously acting on a tidbit from Nietzsche: *The Danger in Happiness.* — "Everything now turns out best for me. I now love every fate: — who would like to be my fate?" (*Apophthegms and Interludes*, No. 103).

21. Most likely an allusion to an actual person, as during this phase, it was common practice to place fantastical persons in actual situations or actual persons in fantastical situations.

22. The illustration also represents various states of being. The student of art should be particularly cautious of interpreting such depictions without proper background training, as it is often easy to confuse source light with light from another world, as in movies when it is easy to confuse internal sound with external sound.[a] Sometimes the artist, as does the director, plays tricks for symbolic purposes.[b]

a. In cinematic terms, "actual sound" refers to sound which comes from a visible or identifiable source[*] within the film. "Commentative sound" is sound which does not come from an identifiable source within the film but is added for dramatic effect.[**]

b. See footnote 1.

[*] By "identifiable source" it is meant that there exists a presupposition, an understanding that an opposing "unidentifiable source" exists.

[**] By "commentative sound" it is meant that there exists a presupposition, an understanding of a "commentator" who is thereby executing the "commentary."

23. The marginalia are as follows: (1.) So too will we confront the one whom the gods have created for us; (2.) And, alas, it is so; (3.) If this is true, then the implication is that one can not destroy what is feared—the general attributes are embodied elsewhere; (4.) Failure of love to be more than fleeting; (5.) Yes, our hero goes alone; (6.) What is feared takes the shape of a serpent; (7.) This would make a lovely title; (8.) The gifts, of course, are symbolic of spiritual unions; (9.) ha ha!; (10.) Is he speaking of the virgin or a whore?

24. The death would indeed involve lunamoths and lilacs.

25. But in those days, I thought that by believing in magic and miracles, by believing hard enough, harder than anyone on earth, I would be made witness to the sublime. And so, what I was doing on the rooftop was praying. I was praying for the gift of flight, for the black umbrella and the hidden angels to aid me.

26. "... for a child—if one allows the awareness of such entities as guardian angels to be true, then the child MUST, as it is contingent, allow for evil to be real as well. For the sublime world of the good and miraculous necessitates the dark, scary walk down the hall each night ..."

27. Besides the obvious lost marbles or stolen purse or misplaced lottery ticket, the theme of loss preoccupied her even in sleep. The following is from a dream dated in the author's 33rd year:

(But then, I remembered in my dream that this was only a dream and that when you lose something in a dream, when you wake up, you realize it's still there. Of course, the reverse is true as well, as when I dreamt I had silver eyes and wings, but upon waking up, upon looking into the mirror, I discovered brown eyes, no wings. So, in my dream, I woke up from my dream in my dream, thereby correcting the situation on my own.

This reminds me of Kafka's *Trial*, in a passage deleted by the author: "... it is really remarkable that when you wake up in the morning you nearly always find everything in exactly the same place as the evening before.")

28. Ezra Pound: Questing and passive.... / "Ah, poor Jenny's case" ...

29. After my sister and I stared at the magazine, we were, the both of us, afraid to part our legs or even to pee. For months, we were inseparable in the bathroom, but then, we became brave and decided to look for our holes, and if the spider did in fact come out we would kill it.

30. It is odd that she chose not to record this particular dream about E. in her log, but instead made loose notes in her journal and later wrote in a letter to Andy:

> . . . he died again. This time, I refused to accept his death because I could still communicate with him and so I asked him if he had, of late, been walking on water or on air, and he answered "neither." I only began to cry at his funeral, and the mourners, they didn't know that it was I who made them; it was I who glued the dragonflies to the scene and said, "You must read his stories." I woke because in my dream, I had been crying too profusely. I slept again and this time, I dreamt the dream of his resurrection: he arrived in my mailbox wrapped in his fiction and covered with butterflies. I ran around, shouting, "He's not dead!" But he is, you see. The dream wants to tell me that he is dead *to me*. The dream wants to inform me not to be fooled by pretty packages, that in matters of correspondence, the body is tragically absent.

31. Never assume that the actors are "sticking to the script." It is recommended that students engaged in cinema studies consult the original scripts and make notes of alterations. Sometimes the director orders last-minute changes. Sometimes too, when one speaks, it is never as one had intended. The student should take note and reconcile the irony that exists between "what should have been"[c] and "what is."[d]

c. " . . . when you see him you will be glad; you will love him . . . and he will never forsake you. This is the meaning of the dream." (G.)[*]

d. "Although I should go in sorrow and in pain, with sighing and with weeping, still I must go." (G.)[*]

[*] This particular footnote is imagined as being elucidated by a future editor.

32. *Genesis* 37:5.2 "And J. dreamed a dream, and she told it her brethren: and they hated her yet the more." 37:8.222 "And they hated her yet the more for her dreams, and for her words." 37:20.7519 "Come now therefore, and let us slay her, and cast her into some pit, and we will say, Some evil beast hath devoured her: and we shall see what will become of her dreams." 40:8.4ii-ixvc5yktg/89.:3lbπ∞ "And they said unto her, You have dreamed a dream, and there is no interpreter of it."

33. I wish he had said "in language there are only *distances*." I've discovered, while watching butterflies mate, that time and metaphor, tragically, are contingent upon each other. For the non-sentient being, there is no time (only eternity). The experience of time translates itself into language, and language translates itself into distance, which translates itself into longing, which is the realization of time. Yes, ironically, it seems as if I've only discovered that the prick was correct. All the same, how sad and strange that I, Jenny Boully, should be the sign of a signifier or the signifier of a sign, moreover, the sign of a signifier searching for the signified.

34. This was corrected in the second edition by the author. In the original, she wrote: "Prayer is merely a hopeful form of apostrophe."

35. I was the lonely tripod. I was the empty cup of tea left behind.
36. The particular nursery rhyme was "Stopping the Swing":

> Die, pussy, die,
> Shut your little eye;
> When you wake,
> Find a cake—
> Die, pussy, die.

37. Hamlet must have slept in a similar bed, for in Act II, Scene ii, he says, "O God, I could be bounded in a nutshell, and count myself a king of infinite space — were it not that I have bad dreams."

38. It was the suspicion that he was reconstructed and retold from ethereal ponderings occurring in some heaven or other that made me want to sleep next to him.

39. It is because of distance, this need, this trying to show you again that I am something else or other, something that could transcribe for you completely whatever it is that your being is refusing to be let known.

40. This letter was never found.

41. I thought about it late and then early again this morning, why it is that we lay the book down in the middle of reading it (or else clutch it to us) and stare off, as if to assimilate the beauty found *there* and integrate it within the *here*—to keep it *here*—to make it, so to say, real.

42. Actually, he would never read her letters that way. Dated in her 25th year:

   ... & yet why do I keep rereading what I have written, attempting to sur- .
mise what you might be inferring, wondering if you will understand me, hop-
ing that you will fall in love with *something* I've written here & thus fall in love
with me? If I were to turn this life into a movie, we'd all be under bridges, then
under tables, then under water, then in the belly of a sperm whale, all the
while speaking of sky; moreover, we'd wear mourning veils, heavy coats, silk
gloves & communicate solely through quill pens & carrier pigeons. If I were
to turn these love letters into a book, the inscription would be by Barthes, &
it would say: *To know that one does not write for the other, to know that these
things I am going to write will never cause me to be loved by the one I love (the
other), to know that writing compensates for nothing, sublimates nothing, that
it is precisely* there *where you are not—this is the beginning of writing.* If this
were a cartoon, you would be a giraffe & I'd be a mouse & we'd live in a
sycamore-leaf shaped house & we'd fight all the time, that is, when you could
hear me, your head being so high up, so far off; I'd sleep in your little alarm
clock, sing a morning song for you, chew holes in your favorite socks, hide my
best straw and bits of yarn in your breast pockets, let you use my tail to mark
your places in books ...

43. The cartographer, in this case, purposely placed the "X" in an obvious, yet incorrect location. The treasure actually rested towards the northeastern edge of the dark wood, 967 paces over the creek away from the side door of the mill house, past 240 cow flops, over 90 large rocks, in the grove of the 540 lilac blossoms where 473 bumble bees seek whatever it is they seek in the air where 1,601 pebbles were tossed.

44. The veil that concealed the sacred of sacreds.

45. In the prop room, she found the collection of butterflies, fossilized bones, her mother's hairbrush, bedsheets belonging to a past love, an earring she lost when she was ten, and a box containing letters which X would compose to her until her death.

46. *Ibid.*, p. xliv.

47. In this case, it was not the *deus ex machina* who was responsible, but rather a certain type of *zeitgeist*.

48. It was after this incident that the leaves began eavesdropping.

49. Recall the question given on the evaluation:

TRUE or FALSE:
When I am alone, I often feel the comforting presence of someone or something nearby that I cannot see but can see me.

50. The package arrived with the following note:

The circuit board is an AM transmitter that basically serves as a small radio station—it propagates signals over a certain frequency (which can be selected). The transmitter, due to some recent modifications, can no longer receive a signal, but it can still send one out. All components have been smashed —the tuner being the only one that was attempted to be repaired. The corners have been broken off, but no vital components are missing.

51. Underneath the covers, the message would always be different: the white bird flying overhead would reveal itself as an emblem of hope; a sigh would be a sign of white flowers held while wearing a white dress; a shiver would be interpreted to mean a shaking of spring leaves, blossoms, or rain; her name, sounding from his mouth, would mean whatever the dream wished it to mean.

52. J.'s famous dream occurred in 1209. In her dream, she spied the moon and it was missing a part.

53. "I wish to question you concerning the living and the dead, how shall I find the life for which I am searching?"

54. When her hair had grown long, she knew the time had come to greet him again. In addition to appendices "Rebirth" and "Phoenix," see also *Gilgamesh*, Part 3: "When you are dead she will let her hair grow long for your sake, she will wear a lion's pelt and wander through the desert . . . The dream was marvelous but the terror was great; we must treasure the dream whatever the terror."

55. When I heard that she was planning to move to Europe, a great panic rose within me and immediately I began scheming ways to accumulate money with which I too could take the trip and follow the great poet.

56. Generally, this symbolizes not the inexplicable, but rather the understood, as in *missing*, as in *variable*; therefore, it is standard practice to plug in possibilities or substitutions in order to discover solutions to one's problem set.

57. Recall that sometimes the world *is* violet and amass with wanderers, and a woman in white, long sought, appears innocent, as if in a pin-up in which anticipation and promise grope one another.

58. In the original production, Boully was positioned stage center, the vase contained lilacs, not violets, the hills spread out like fallen pears, and _____ was originally cast to play the role of _____ who, in the original production, entered on the cue of broken glass to ask if she would _____ him. The addition of black curtains, which replaced the billowing, transparent ones, was made in the year _____. Del Vecchio contends this is indicative of Boully's growing apprehension of _____. The change in the set design was intended to symbolize the changes made in the dialogue, as _____ would no longer be asking if she would _____ him, but if she was okay with just _____ing him.

59. Not the celestial body, but the cleaning agent, which was commonly used to scrub toilets and dislodge mildew from cracks and crevices.

60. From her travel journal, written during the five years of her self-imposed "nun-hood":

> ... I tried to make myself pure by giving up touching myself, that part of myself that my mother used to call a turtle and then a clam. But there I was, under the blue mosquito net, blue, not unlike the color of my dreams. The cocks were crowing for morning and I began; I began having to start this dream over again. (Perhaps when the cock crows, it signifies only the crowing of the cock and nothing more. Perhaps the aubade is, in fact, only a convention. I should be so free.)

61. The dogwoods were especially lovely that year.

62. This particular question she always answered, "No comment."

63. July 8, 1976.

64. The fact that she named her imaginary child Zeno should be considered along with the following excerpts. The last time she saw E., they met in New York on her birthday. She wrote on a series of postcards to Andy, and these are given in the order in which they arrived in his mailbox:

(POSTCARD 4): Therefore, place does not exist." But he was mistaken, Andy, terribly mistaken. Moving through these streets, flying away from E. time and time again, measuring "out my life with coffee spoons," I harbor a sure sense always of always existing in the plane of "here" while E. is always "there," always "elsewhere." I miss you. I wish I were not here, & I remain, as ever, yours, etc., JB

(POSTCARD 2): of hotel sheets. I am already envying them their placement of ornaments on Christmas trees and their china and silver sets. At my age, a woman should be wary of having children. Zeno of Elea is known to have said, "If place exists, where is it? For everything that exists is in a place. Therefore, place is in a place.

(POSTCARD 1): My dearest Andy, today, I turned 36 and summertime in NY is no longer pink candlelight. My eyes carry the crumbling veins of autumn leaves, and E., who is 40, has just confessed to asking a 20 yr old to marry him, to which she replied yes and that this must be the last of our time together as lovers who can share no secrets anyhow under cover

(POSTCARD 3): This goes on to infinity.

65. It is futile for the student engaged in cinema studies to write a paper on any aspect of film without first explicating the significance of the fortune teller's answer to Antonio when he inquires again about his stolen bicycle: she says to him, "Either you find it now or you never will."

66. Or whatever the translation might be. As a verb, it is understood to mean *to long for* _____ (*despite one's logical reasoning which intuits there is nothing to be gained) in expectation of its fulfillment.* As a noun, however, a source and reason for this longing is posited in the very definition.

67. Consider too that according to Euclid's assumptions, a straight line extends infinitely. Furthermore, the fifth postulate posits that space is enchanted, incipient and capable of collapse and disappearance all the same. Johann Bolyai, 21 and bound within notebook after notebook, over a singular desk and many candlewicks, wrote to his father:

> It is now my definite plan to publish a work on parallels as soon as I can complete and arrange the material and an opportunity presents itself; at the moment I still do not clearly see my way through, but the path which I have followed gives positive evidence that the goal will be reached, if it is at all possible; I have not quite reached it, but I have discovered such wonderful things that I was amazed, and it would be an everlasting piece of bad fortune if they were lost. When you, my dear Father, see them, you will understand; at present, I can say nothing except this: that out of nothing, I have created a strange new universe. All that I have sent you previously is like a house of cards in comparison with a tower.

68. Actually, what she most desired was someone who would pay close attention to details—the type of person who would never misplace a comma or misspell a word, who would point out and love all those things she deemed lovable about herself such as the manner in which she wrote ampersands, the two freckles on her left hand, the golden highlights in her hair and other such trifling matters; secretly, therefore, she desired someone who might allow himself to be engaged in the world of platitudes, yet she always sought out men who liked to (o)pen the heaviest of books and read them whorishly, jumping from one author to the next, abandoning one for another, starting one and never finishing, forgetting the minute yet most important details and the names of characters, folding corners instead of using bookmarks, writing pretentious marginalia, pretending to have read certain books when engaged in cocktail-party-conversations, reading certain books only to be able to say they have read them and without want or love, etc.

69. According to legend, it would rise from the bog on the night of a full moon in search of.

70. *John* 20:9 "For as yet they knew not the scripture, that he must rise again from the dead." 20:11.6.10.99 "But she stood without at the sepulchre weeping: and as she wept, she stooped down, and *looked* into the sepulchre"ᵉ 20:13 "And they say unto her, Woman, why weepest thou? She saith unto them, Because they have taken away my Lord, and I know not where they have laid him." 20:14.21401 "And when she had thus said, she turned herself back, and saw _____ standing, and knew not that it was _____." 20:15.33333 . . . "_____ saith unto her, Woman, why weepest thou? whom seekest thou?"

   e. Not a sepulchre, but an envelope; not an envelope, but a door; not a door, but a fire escape.*

   * The inclusion of this note was deemed necessary by the editor, lest false surmises† lead to injuries.

   † "And there is a third nature, which is space and is eternal, and admits not of destruction and provides a home for all created things, and is apprehended, when all sense is absent, by a kind of spurious reason, and is hardly real — which we, beholding as in a dream, say of all existence that it must of necessity be in some place and occupy a space, but that what is neither in heaven nor in earth has no existence. Of these and other things of the same kind, relating to the true and waking reality of nature, we have only this dreamlike sense, and we are unable to cast off sleep and determine the truth about them" (52*b–c*).

71. She demanded to see my journals, saying that she could, from my personal writings, determine whether I was a true poet or an impostor. This was the first time I lied to the great poet: I told her that I didn't keep a journal. The truth, however, was that I was keeping a journal, but discovered that writing was related to obsession. I knew it was unhealthy to obsess over the great poet; therefore, I stopped writing. With no voice, I could not make tangible my obsession, thereby ignored it, thereby did not have to live with the physical proof of the shame of it. She said that I was insipid. She said that I should groom[f] my nails.[g]

> f. *groom* as in *marriage*.
> g. *nails* as in *fuck*.

72. There is no documentation that she was afraid of bears, per se; however, the bear in this dream is only contextually a bear:

> . . . so this bear came in through my window and I decided that I wasn't going to be afraid of it but that I'd have sex with it and so the bear became more and more human. Then, as a man, it positioned my pelvis in a certain way because he wanted me to look as he ate me out. I didn't want to look. I didn't feel comfortable, so I just pretended that it felt good so that I could close my eyes when really it didn't feel good at all. I remember packing a suitcase because I got tired of waiting for X and decided that I would go to New York all by myself.

73. See also *tragic irony*.[h]

> h. The great poet, despite all her attempts to construct an original semblance of reality, died surrounded by clichés: her body was set adrift where the land meets the sea, her boat was loaded with red roses, a bystander whispered something about *Annabel Lee*, and fog, drizzle, and mist entered the scenery so that one could not see to where her death boat drifted.

74. "Because of the finitude of this type of travel, one should pack lightly, as words have different connotations according to different witnesses, as all people do not hear the same note of music at the same time, nor do events that appear simultaneous *visually* seem to be audibly simultaneous.

"Light and prayer also have finite speeds, so we never see an instantaneous snapshot of eternity. The flight of light is so swift that within a single lifetime we obtain *effectively* an instantaneous snapshot, but this is certainly not the case astronomically. We see the moon as it was just over a second ago, and the sun as it was about 8 min ago. At the same time, we see the stars by light that departed from them years ago, and the other galaxies as they were millions of lifetimes in the past. We do not observe the world about us at an instant in time, but rather we see different possible lives about us as different *events* in spacetime.

"Relatively moving observers do not even agree on the order of events . . ." (*Ibid.*, p. 523).

75. Because the weather and landscape were forever shifting and birds gave birth to new birds that birthed new birds *ad infinitum*, this passage is, historically, inaccurate. The main argument, however, remains unaffected.

76. When the protagonist happens upon the crime scene, when she stumbles into the prop room, when she reads the work of the great poet, and most importantly, when she holds the letter up to the sun to read between the lines, the author is supplying examples of *dramatic irony*.[i]

   i. "Dramatic irony usually refers to a situation in a play wherein a character, whose knowledge is limited, says, does, or encounters something of greater significance than she knows" (*Ibid.*, p. 29).

77. For types of drama, *see: absurd, literature of the; atmosphere; chronicle plays; commedia dell'arte; comedy; comedy of humours; drama of sensibility; epic theater; expressionism; folk drama; heroic drama; masque; melodrama; miracle plays, morality plays, and interludes; mummer's play; pantomime and dumb show; pastoral; problem play; satire; sentimental comedy; tragedy; tragicomedy.*

78. ". . . for spectators at a circus to find themselves suddenly beholding a greater and more horrific show than they had paid for" (*Ibid.*, p. 30).

79. She wrote about this particular postcard in her journal:

> ... Why should I be the one responsible for explanations? [illegible] accused me of speaking in cryptic codes and waxing poetic. But why should I waste language, which has never done [illegible] and me any good? Why should I waste language, when one sentence says all that needs to be said, says where I've been, whom I've seen, what I'm doing, whom I'm missing, and whom I wish were there? ...

Dated two years later:

> ... The postcard was returned to me, covered with a multitude of postmarks, some from as far as Japan and Madagascar. Apparently, it had gotten lost all over the world before reaching me. The original inscription[j] is hardly legible; however, I can still make out [illegible]'s handwriting underneath my own. It says: "what the fuck is this supposed to mean?" Thus, the last words of our relationship; thus, once more, the crossing of oceans and years to reach, once more, the closure of confusion.

j. Alas, it was hardly legible, so much so that we are incapable of discerning what it says.

80. 71.10. τών αφανών, *of the missing.* — 14. σημα, *sepulchre.* — 72.7. λόγον, *oration.* — 15. δόκησις της άληθείας, *the appearance* (or *impression*) *of truthfulness.* The sentence means, that people are very distrustful of an orator, however truthful he may be. — 17, 18. τι ἐνδεεστέρως . . . δηλουσθαι, *that something is expressed too imperfectly.* — πρὸς ἁ, *in comparison with what.* — ἄπειρος, sc. νομίσειε. — 18, 19. ἐστιν ἁ, *some things* (C. 559. a; G. 152, N. 2; H. 812). — και πλεονάξεσθαι , *are even exaggerated.* — 21. ες όσον, *as far as.* — 23. τω . . . αύτων, *but whatever surpasses these* (C. 456; G. 184, 2; H. 595, b). — 73.21. ξηλούση, *copy.* — 74.2, 3, 4. ουδε . . . προστιθέμενοι, *nor adopting moroseness, which, though harmless, is painful to see.* — 6. τών belongs with όντων, and, like νόμων, depends on ακροάσει. — αεί, *at the time.* — 7. ακροάσει, *because we obey* (dat. of cause). — αυτων depends on μάλιστα (C. 420, c; G. 168; H. 559). — 8. κεινται, *are enacted.* — 11. γνώμη, *mind.* — 12. νομίξοντες, *maintaining* (lit. *establishing as custom, believing in*). νομίξειν with the dat. has much the same force as χρησθαι. — 76.26, 27. των δ' . . . βλάψει, *while the truth shall mar the conception* (derived from the poet) *of the deeds.* — 77.1. δικαιουντες, κ, τ, λ., *resolving not to be deprived of it.* — 3. πάντα τινά, *each one.* — 4, 5. διδασκαλίαν τε ποιούμενος, *for the sake of showing* (lit. *imparting instruction:* the part. denotes purpose). — 24, 25. το αφανές, *the uncertainty.* — 78.1. απηλλάησαν, *they were removed.* — 4, 5. διάνοιαν, *spirit.* — σκοπουντας λόγω, contrasted with έρλω θεωμένους, below. — 6, 8. ην . . . ένεστιν : parenthetic. — πρὸς . . . ειδότας, *to you who know it full well.* — 9. έργω, *in fact,* i.e. *as it really is.* — 11, 13. αισχυνόμενοι, *open to shame.* — 13, 14. πείρα του σφαλέιησαν, *they failed in any attempt.* — 15, 16. καλλιστον έρανον, *a most noble offering,* i.e. their lives. έρανος means primarily a mutual contribution to an entertainment, like our picnic. — 79.16–18. τέκνωσιν ποιεισθαι = τεκνοποιειν. — ιδία — ληθη — τισιν ἔσονται, *will cause some of you, individually, to forget.*

81. Besides the need to act out various life-or-death scenarios, children of every culture engage in a variation of *hide-and-go-seek*.

82. Lacan: "... _____ is both an obstacle to remembering, and a making present of the closure of the _____, which is the act of missing the right meeting just at the right moment."

83. Gilgamesh also lost a bicycle: "Gilgamesh, where are you hurrying to? You will never find that life for which you are looking" . . . "I found a sign and I have lost it."

84. Like all men trained in the investigative sciences, he was schooled in skepticism; hence his refusal to completely discard the old theory of despair in favor of the one full of promises, on grounds that he lacked "convincing evidence."

85. They would be unable to realize it then, but later, in the other world, they would look back and realize that the monuments were attempts to create a reality that transpired at the speed of prayer.

86. Guarded.

87. To properly protect one's hard drive, one should take great care to not open attachments[k] from unknown users.

k. Consider *love* here.

88. Perhaps what she was trying to get at was this: "I am awakened to myself and my unhappiness just as my interest has become most intense. The audience begins to clap impatiently" (*In Dreams Begin Responsibilities*, Delmore Schwartz).

89. "I would find what I wanted to do, and I would stick with it. In my childhood home, the silverware laid in drawers, heaped together like his matched loves."

90. An alias.

91. Despite all his expertise in mimicry, the movie director could not put _____ back together again; moreover, he could not properly render the realism of the crime scene: notice the microphone dangling in the upper-left corner of the frame; the blood which appeared before the kill; the lipstick on the antagonist's left check when the protagonist clearly kissed him on his right; the visible strings of all the flying things; the wax and Popsicle sticks comprising the wings; the letter read before the envelope was unsealed; the death certificate found and forged before the death; the cicadas leaving their ghosts on fences and vines; the appearance of butterflies before the splitting of cocoons; the outline of the body drawn in chalk before the collapse of the victim; the ill-timed street lights; the collection in the detective's book of clues of evidence before the crime was even committed; and the supposedly random appearance of the man in the fedora offering flowers when, in the previous scene, he had discarded them in the river.

92. "Audiences have, for decades, been entranced by her films; however, when she made a cameo appearance (falling from the sky in the manner of Icarus), ironically, the audience, as well as film critics, failed to take notice."

93. The footnote in question was actually from Jacques Derrida, in his book *Dissemination*, in the essay *Plato's Pharmacy*, in *Part I*, in section 3. *The Filial Inscription: Theuth, Hermes, Thoth, Nabû, Nebo*. It is reproduced here in its entirety:

42. Vandier, p. 230. Cryptography, medicinal magic, and the figure of the serpent are in fact intertwined in an astonishing folk tale transcribed by G. Maspéro in *Les Contes populaires de l'Egypte ancienne* (Paris: E. Guilmoro, 1911). It is the tale of Satni-Khamois and the mummies. Satni-Khamois, the son of a king, "spent his days running about the metropolis of Memphis so as to read the books written in sacred script and the books of the *Double House of Life*. One day a nobleman came along and made fun of him. — 'Why are you laughing at me?' The nobleman said: — 'I am not laughing at you; but can I help laughing when you spend your time here deciphering writings that have no powers? If you really wish to read effective writing, come with me; I will send you to the place where you will find the book which Thoth himself has written with his own hand and which will place you just below the gods. There are two formulas written in it: if you recite the first, you will charm the sky, the earth, the world of night, the mountains, the waters; you will understand what the birds of the sky and the reptiles are all saying, as they are; you will see the fish, for a divine force will make them rise to the surface of the water. If you read the second formula, even if you are in the grave you will reassume the form you had on earth; even shall you see the sun rising in the sky, and its cy-

cle, and the moon in the form it has when it appears.' Satni cried; 'By my life!
let me know what you wish and I will have it granted you; but take me to the
place where I can find the book!' The nobleman said to Satni: 'The book in
question is not mine. It is in the heart of the necropolis, in the tomb[l] of Neno-
ferkeptah, son of king Minebptah. . . . Take great heed not to take this book
away from him, for he would have you bring it back, a pitchfork and a rod in
his hand, a lighted brazier on his head. . . .' Deep inside the tomb, light was
shining out of the book. The doubles of the king and of his family were beside
him, 'through the virtues of the book of Thoth.' . . . All this was repeating it-
self. Nenoferkeptah had already himself lived Satni's story. The priest had told
him: 'The book in question is in the middle of the sea of Coptos, in an iron
casket.[m] The iron casket is inside a bronze casket; the bronze casket is inside
a casket of cinnamon wood; the casket of cinnamon wood is inside a casket of
ivory and ebony. The casket of ivory and ebony is inside a silver casket. The
silver casket is inside a golden casket, and the book is found therein. {Scribe's
error? the first version I consulted had consigned or reproduced it; a later edi-
tion of Maspéro's book pointed it out in a note: "The scribe has made a mis-
take here in his enumeration. He should have said: *inside* the iron casket is . . .

l. Not a tomb but an envelope; not an envelope, but a door; not a door, but
a fire escape.

m. Not a casket but an envelope; not an envelope, but a window; not a win-
dow, but a sigh.

etc." (Item left as evidence for a logic of inclusion).} And there is a schoene {in Ptolemy's day, equal to about 12,000 royal cubits of 0.52m} of serpents, scorpions of all kinds, and reptiles around the casket in which the book lies, and there is an immortal serpent coiled around the casket in question.'" After three tries, the imprudent hero kills the serpent, drinks the book dissolved in beer, and thus acquires limitless knowledge. Thoth goes to Ra to complain, and provokes the worst of punishments.

Let us note, finally before leaving the Egyptian figure of Thoth, that he possesses, in addition to Hermes of Greece, a remarkable counterpart in the figure of Nabu, son of Marduk. In Babylonian and Assyrian mythology, "Nabu is essentially the son-god and, just as Marduk eclipses his father, Ea, we will see Nabu usurping Marduk's place." (E. Dhorme, *Les Religions de Babylonie et d'Assyrie* {Paris: Presses Universitaires de France}, pp. 150 ff.) Marduk, the father of Nabu, is the sun-god. Nabu, "lord of the reed," "creator of writing," "bearer of the tables of the fates of the gods," sometimes goes ahead of his father from whom he borrows the symbolic instrument, the *marru*. "A votive object made of copper, uncovered in Susa, representing 'a snake holding in its mouth a sort of pall,' was marked with the inscription 'the marru of the god Nabu'" (Dhorme, p. 155). Cf. also M. David, *Les Dieux et le Destin en Babylonie* (Paris: P.U.F., 1949), pp. 86 ff.

One could spell out one by one the points of resemblance between Thoth and the biblical Nabu (Nebo).

94. The great poet advised her to always keep a journal, especially in matters of love, as being in love means one will participate in irrational behavior. A journal, the great poet guaranteed, will provide something explanatory for later, while gaps of time when one failed to write would mean that one had no record of the affair—love with no proof of purchase, and therefore, no hopes of redemption or exchanges.

95. Surely, no reader will fail to recognize this opening line.

96. Horace, 1. *Epistles* I.1.98–99.

97. The following was written on the penultimate page of a journal full of quotes which she called "clues": *Nehemiah* 6:3 "And I sent messengers unto them, saying, I am doing a great work, so that I can not come down: why should the work cease, whilest I leave it, and come down to you?"; J.C.: " . . . the deeds of victory are rendered, not in lifelike, but in dreamlike figurations; for the point is not that such-and-such was done on earth; the point is that, before such-and-such could be done on earth, this other, more important, primary thing had to be brought to pass within the labyrinth that we all know and visit in our dreams."

97.1. "It was not I that revealed the secret of the gods; the wise man learned it in a dream" (G.).

98. "You will never find the life for which you are searching."

99. Except, perhaps, for poets and prostitutes.

100. Before being moved to empathy, the reader should keep in mind that the night did not last long; moreover, it demanded that she return all that she had stolen.[n]

n. In the morning, the doves cooed their *fuck-yous*. And she departed, taking the wrong baggage, the wrong flight of stairs. Over the fire escape, the dress fluttered in the misdirected wind. Because he never said the word, the bits and pieces of her: lipstick and rose petals, sugar-spoons and pink envelopes, ended up in the wrong pockets. And damn-it-all-to-hell if someone didn't, overnight, uproot and replant the road signs in all the most-traveled but wrong intersections. In the cathedral, the font was never so wanton, yet it liked that dipping of fingers again and again, and the candles were so whorish in their sharing of flames.

101. The omens were as follows:

>—the black bird perched on a snowman in twilight;
>—the black brassiere under the wedding dress;
>—the open mouth, spreading forever as the sea and without
>a CAUTION sign, panting like bad sin and hurrying to it;
>—the grackles which cackled like spinsters, a snare sounding
>of carnivals, gypsy songs.

102. If the window is open, then true. If the door was abruptly shut, then false. If the villanelle was blonde, then add five points to your answer. If she was drinking a dirty martini, subtract 60 points for fear. If you forgot her name, wait out a turn. If love, then the ace of spades: for everything else, re-shuffle and deal again.

103. Lewis Carroll, from *The Hunting of the Snark*:

> "I engage with the Snark—every night after dark—
> In a dreamy delirious fight:
> I serve it with greens in those shadowy scenes,
> And I use it for striking a light;
>
> "But if ever I meet with a Boojum, that day,
> In a moment (of this I am sure),
> I shall softly and suddenly vanish away—
> And the notion I cannot endure!"

104. Fade in on the image of an aperture being adjusted from a sigh to a gasp to a pinpoint, from the POV of the cameraman. Voice over to indistinguishable whispering coupled with slight murmurings given over to faintness. Aperture enlarges, and through it, one merely spies hands, screwing in a light bulb. Zoom out: our protagonist is on a fire escape; the night is Payne's Grey. The stairs are unstable. Jump cut to a hand on the light chain, tugging to turn it off. Fade out. Voices cease.

105. [All the films of this epoch were met with inevitable failure: the jump cuts always appeared irregular, intrusive, and rickety; always a small light leak would blotch the film; somehow, sequences were spliced together in incorrect order (moreover, the splicing tape would show); always, the projector would skip at the climax of the film; and sadly none of the reels survived, all having melted due to overheating.][o]

> o. Consider *love* here.

106. That he gave her this particular flower as opposed to that particular flower, that he presented it to her in such and such a way, that the cows' behavior was odd indeed and cow flops were unavoidable, that although it was a pleasant day, the chilly night air moved slyly in, and that they disagreed about the shade of the dusk sky should not fool the casual reader into believing that the scene was set in such and such a way at random and without purpose. After all, in the editing room, the editor often wields greater power than the director.

107.

108. Although the argument is convincing and its logic flawless, we must keep in mind that during this stage, the author also professed to having been in a deep coma and taking to walking and talking in her sleep.

109. "But a trace in the strict sense disturbs the order of the world. It occurs by overprinting. Its original signifyingness is sketched out in, for example, the fingerprints left by someone who wanted to wipe away his traces and commit a perfect crime."

110. Joseph Campbell: "It is the realm that we enter in sleep. We carry it within ourselves forever. All the ogres and secret helpers of our nursery are there, all the magic of childhood."

111. See also Federico Fellini's 8½, paying close attention to the meaning of *Asa Nisa Masa*. Perhaps if our protagonist had access to the right words, she could have navigated through the painting, which, in the dark each night, revealed itself as a passage.

112. Read the onset of menstruation along with the following: ". . . a little brook, the redness of which still makes me shudder . . . which the sinful women share among them" (Dante, *Inferno*).

113. "It is getting so dark that I can scarcely go on writing; and my brush is all worn out. Yet I should like to add a few things before I end" (Sei Shōnagon, *The Pillow Book*).

114. Understandably so, however: "Any two freely falling bodies,[p] independent of their composition and internal structure, will follow identical paths.[q] This similarity of behavior of all types of objects is called an *equivalence principle.*[r]

"Einstein broadened this equivalence principle and as a consequence reached sweeping conclusions about the very fabric of space and time. The basic postulate of Einstein's equivalence principle is that life in a freely falling laboratory is indistinguishable from, and hence equivalent to, life with no gravity. . . .[p] `

". . . Appearances are misleading.[q] There *is* a force.[r]* Neither the Shuttle nor the astronauts are *really* weightless, for they continually fall around the Earth, pulled by its gravity. But since all fall together—Shuttle, astronauts, wrench, and pencil—within the Shuttle all _____ appear to be absent" (*Ibid.*, p. 521–522).

p. Consider *love* here.

q. Consider how she remained and he strayed.

r. Then maybe, perhaps, one falls while the other falls not?

* There is a _____.

115. The following is a found fragment addressed to the great poet, dated two years after the death of the great poet:

. . . It was my cunt, too — not the velvet one, of course, but the center one with the hanged man attached to it. That same summer, my sister and I turned detective and held the spy glass over the ants and discovered they were busy planning hoaxes. Everything I do, I do because I know I am dying. My most favorites of things are optical illusions. We don't become senile or "lose our minds," it's just that as we get older, we have more to think of in less time — we must think of more in a compressed amount of time. I think I know now what you've tried to teach me: poetry is an instant, an instant in which transcendence is achieved, where a miracle occurs and all of one's knowledge, experiences, memories etc. are obliterated into awe. Is anything I say real? And by real, I mean *sincere* — or is everything an attempt to procure love? I know now why the line breaks: it is because something dies, and elsewhere, is born again . . .

116. 550.28. *a rarre-shew-box:* a peep-show.

117. The illustration for this scene deserves careful study.

118. *Exodus* 33:20–23.

119. Although our protagonist lacked the key, she spied through the key-hole and beheld the costumers, their mouths full of pins and needles, busying themselves with the taking of the sky's measurements and debating the various advantages of the memory of royal blue over pale purple. Finally, they settled on Payne's Grey.

120. Catch them off guard: turn your head fast enough, and you can glimpse them with their paintbrushes and nails, their rolls and rolls of backdrop.

121. We are unable to determine whether the exact wording has a source.

122. The crux of the matter is that behind the curtain, there exists the stage; however, beyond the stage is the area referred to as "back stage"; furthermore, beyond the area referred to as "back stage," there is the "green room"; and finally, there are the "wings" through which actors enter and exit.

123. "The connotation of the word, Stephen said, is rather vague. Aquinas uses a term which seems to be inexact. It baffled me for a long time. It would lead you to believe that he had in mind symbolism or idealism, the supreme quality of beauty being a light from another world, the idea of which the matter is but the shadow, the reality of which it is but the symbol. I thought he might mean that *claritas* is the artistic discovery and representation of the divine purpose in anything or a force of generalisation which would make the esthetic image a universal one, make it outshine its proper conditions" (*A Portrait of the Artist as a Young Man*, p. 213).

124. Although the polygraph would record this statement as true, the judge would order that this evidence be thrown out on the grounds that it had been "tampered with."

125. When we are afraid, we often react to fear by pretending to be what we are not; take for instance, the act of mimicry: a lunamoth will splay her wings to have her predator take her for some fierce, nocturnal beast.

126. This concerns the audience in the dark; moreover, the fade-out is necessary to distill the correct level of confusion: *are they making love or is someone being murdered?*

127. 1606 SHAKES. *Ant. & Cl.* IV. vi. 37, I will go seeke Some Ditch wherein to dye.

128. From Cantos XIII:

> ... "And even I can remember
> A day when the historians left blanks in their writings,
> I mean for things they didn't know,
> But that time seems to be passing."

128½. He never did find it, although she swore to him that she had in fact hidden it somewhere. We are surmising that the message in question is the following, still sealed in its pink envelope, written in the author's handwriting, and found tucked inside E.'s copy of Euclid's *Elements:*

> This
> is the departure strip,
> the dream-road. Whoever built it
> left numbers, words and arrows.
> He had to leave in a hurry.
> —R.L.

(E: re: it's all *here*. Happy birthday. love, miss jenny)

129. Filmmaker Lousine Shamamian suggests that the fade-out leaving the sound of wings knocking against glass is meant to imply that the protagonist grew weary of impersonating herself.

130. The game was actually caught after the end of the official hunting season. The following note was found stuffed in the barrel of the rifle:

> Don't mistake the hunter for the great spirit: one is sincere and truly dies once a year—the other puts on such garments when he aims to *use* them; one wants to lay you down beside him and witness the colors of the changing show—the other wants to shoot his load into you; one wants to love and admire you from afar, from a leaf cell or a fleck of snow—the other wants to spread and mount you.

131. ". . . all women secretly desire to be sacrifices; they long to be 'the chosen one.'"

132. The director introduced the third person by placing him stage left, right by the oldest of willow trees where Boully was sitting, contemplating the river; however, in order to create the correct level of surprise on Boully's part, the director kept this character hidden until opening night; the result was the most convincing of performances in that Boully was totally out of character.

133. Emmanuel Levinas: ". . . the whole weight of being can be resolved into a play of inwardness and stand on the brink of illusion, so rigorous is the adequation [sic]. The apparition of being is possibly but appearance. The shadow is taken for a prey; the prey is let loose for the shadow" (*The Trace of the Other*).

134. "As in the dark month, the month of shadows, so without him there is no light . . . this was the meaning of your dream."

135. "You had better go inside; it's getting dark."

136. The onset of puberty *would* mean the death of eternity: with menstruation, she would know that a month had passed; when it ceased altogether, she would know, for certain, that the years had elapsed.

137. Even so, I go my own way, following the drifts of the hourglass, laurelled with lightening-blue bumblebees, at the foot of the lunamoth-winged sky, as on the bottom of the whale-born sea.

138. The response from the great poet was written on a postcard:

> J: You've failed once more in that a good poem is never tidy—never let on that you went through great pains to get your lipstick just right; lines should break like kamikazes; you should be beautiful in your slovenliness; you should be enticing in your near-suicide.

139. It was unearthed from its burial site and auctioned off three years later. The proprietor spoke rather vaguely of its contents: _____, _____, _____, and a used _____; he was, rightly so, disappointed, thinking that the box contained gold or jewels or money. Tristram, who could not stand for such ill use of the author's most dear of possessions, offered his life's savings in exchange for the chest and its contents: what he found were all the letters, among others, that he had composed to her; a photograph he took of the author at 24; her journals; a map of _____; an itinerary for _____; a moth-infested wedding dress sized 4; and a ticket stub to *The Real Thing*.

140. The found fragments of the letters,[s] composed to E. on uncertain dates, are as follows:

... perhaps not — & I suppose I'd understand if you disagree —. My sources tell me that beyond the cloudiness, behind the blurs — you may or may not be [illegible] — this much remains to be seen. I understand manna now, E. It means eat up the moment. In the desert, in drought, in famine, there falls manna & in the Bible, they call this a miracle. In those rare moments when I am not re-membering my past or given over to anxiety of future occurrences, I eat my manna & experience a miracle indeed. My sin is that I have so little manna that I try to save it & it is never there. But ... I digress ... I am not torn in the composing, but in the delivery.[t] *Do I dare?* I admire your gentle use of refrain.[u] The geography of our potential recollections keeps expanding. Perhaps it would be more apt if I were the amnesiac. My calendar has very tiny spaces in which to write, so I always have a vague notion of what I need to be doing & when & where. In this world, so many things named *Clementine* — *gone and lost forever*. This, as you must imagine, is a great source of irritation & anguish for me. I am waiting for payday so that I may buy a new one. (I still have the overwhelming desire to tell you everything.) The same state of tragicness forever (?): *I'm not so young but not so very old, / said screwed-up lovely 23. / A final sense of being out in the cold, / unkissed.*[v] I wish you didn't only half

s. These were not among E.'s belongings: we can only surmise that these were not working copies; therefore, he failed to receive them.

t. Perhaps an indication that this was never sent?

u. Perhaps a cryptic way of alluding to the whole affair?*

v. John Berryman.

* If so, should we then consider the various meanings of *refrain*?†

†*n.* A repeated utterance or theme; *v.* To hold oneself back; forbear.

inquire and then hold it all against me. I seem to be cursed with language—by destroying paradise by naming it. I am on a secret game show. I want a new category. The game host is cruel. I act in the manner which I think will, in the end, be more rewarding. I like to think someone is secretly watching and loving me. It makes me feel utterly tragic & cosmic in my emotional proportions. Magical things befall daily. Dare I think [illegible]? I have refused call after call because I truly believe that the journey shouldn't be unless it is magically in-tune with my vision of what a bridge[w] or a spider[x] or a blade of grass[y] should be. In other words, unless I could transform the symbols & metaphors around me & have it be child's play & be understood, then I could come out to play. But, as ever, there was only . . .

[fragment breaks here]

. . . could always find the candy house in the woods, & as I am writing this, however bizarre, cryptic, coded it may be, I know he understands just what I mean. (To be able to think, to obsess, in language, is it the same as recognizing & understanding the distance between sign & signifier? or is it the manner in which the distance becomes obliterated? I do not know.) I keep imagining my mother, outside, cutting roses. The other night, I dreamt of clouds of monarch butterflies and my whole family went out to the back porch to wit-

w. More properly, a narrow, single lane bridge with a caution sign before it.
x. Perhaps of the type that enjoys scaring away little girls?
y. Perhaps an allusion to Frank O'Hara's *Meditations in an Emergency?*[**]

[**] More likely an allusion to Joseph Campbell, as the following was marked off with stars in her book: "Or again: a great temple can be established anywhere . . . Any blade of grass may assume, in myth, the figure of the savior and conduct the questing wanderer into the sanctum sanctorum of his own heart."

ness and one was so huge and I was afraid of it and it was coming towards me and revealed itself as a kite and I do not know what to make of such a dream. By the time this reaches you . . .

[fragment ends here]

. . . is it, or can it ever hope to be sincere? Here, my mother would say that I am looking at it all wrong and truthfully, the dilemma is solved by discovering thus: the inherent sincerity is the cause of the motive; yearning as the extreme manifestation of sincerity. Here is where language can cause me trouble—when everything makes sense if I word it just right & by invoking a false scene. What scares me is reading my journals & I sometimes (always?) sound like a stranger. Is it possible that I can be insincere to myself? To my most intimate, private self? Or is it that sincerity manifests the stranger in me? Or, does the same motive apply not only to the universe, but to the self as well? Is it that to write for the self is to both love & seek love from the self? I know, I must exist quite differently in paper than in person & this worries me, because if this is correct, then I need to ask myself: which self is the most sincere?; which self is the more real?; which self triggers the yearning & thus supplies the motive?; which self, because it either speaks or writes (i.e. it employs language), desires . . .

[fragment cuts off here]

. . . I remember wanting yellow, green, blue. In this scene, in which I have just fallen out of the sky to join you in a realm of color, we [illegible—paper blotched by water?] . . . is a dichotomy connecting a dialectic . . . [illegible] . . . a semblance of present unity w/in present, physical separation . . . [illegible] . . . could any of this have been foreseeable considering that [illegible]

[fragment ends here]

141. The true crux of the matter had little to do with space and passages, but rather with the elements of scenery itself: the lights are waiting to dim, the fuses to blow, the glass to shatter, the curtain to drop, the director, in turn, to apologize for having to cancel the show.

142. If Hamlet was indeed sleeping in a similar bed, then Vladimir Nabokov was bounded in a nutshell similar to Hamlet's. The following excerpt from *Speak, Memory*, written in E.'s handwriting, was pasted into one of her journals: "I have to make a rapid inventory of the universe, just as a man in a dream tries to condone the absurdity of his position by making sure he is dreaming. I have to have all space and all time participate in my emotion, in my mortal love, so that the edge of its mortality is taken off, thus helping me to fight the utter degradation, ridicule, and horror of having developed an infinity of sensation and thought within a finite existence."

143. After the author's death, it was Tristram who went through her various papers and came across the many folders labeled "footnotes." It wasn't until years later, when he was curious as to which papers the footnotes corresponded that Tristram discovered that the "footnotes" were actually daily journals of the author's dreams. Del Vecchio recalls a later audiocassette recording with the author saying, "I have it all worked out. I write down my dreams because I understand them once symbols become written. They're all so sexually charged and I almost always feel ugly in them; they're embarrassing and filthy. But I have it all worked out. No one will know. I've relabeled everything in my study, including my books—you think you're getting Shakespeare, but really, it's astrophysics and cosmology or you open Hesse and you actually get Kierkegaard. I'm not so off am I? But really, I must confess . . ." Del Vecchio, in her words, says, "And then she started going on and on about this Robert Kelly[z] guy."

z. The following excerpt from Robert Kelly's "Edmund Wilson on Alfred de Musset: The Dream" was pasted above the author's various beds in the various places she lived: "Dreams themselves are footnotes. But not footnotes to life. Some other transactions they are so busy annotating all night long."

144. The mastermind of this roller coaster, in an interview, confessed that the goal of his work is to replicate a ride in which participants are scared out of their minds, yet feel the comforting presence of someone there, riding along and watching over them.

145. The photographs were selected from the wrong box: as she never had any children, photograph 34 is unthinkable; photograph 12 is also bogus because in any event, the engagement ring is on the wrong finger; photograph 56 is dated three years before her birth; photograph 108 shows her happy; as she never looked anyone in the eye, photograph 9 must be compiled from one of the other possible lives, because she wouldn't ever think of looking a camera lens in the eye; this goes on to infinity.

146. This situation also contains *cosmic irony* or *irony of fate*: "some Fate with a grim sense of humor seems cruelly to trick a man . . . God, or destiny, or the process of the universe, is represented as though deliberately manipulating events so as to lead the protagonist to false hopes, only to frustrate and mock them" (*Ibid.*, p. 30).

147. J.C.: "Whether dream or myth, in these adventures there is an atmosphere of irresistible fascination about the figure that appears suddenly as a guide, marking a new period, a new stage, in the biography."

148. *Ibid.*, conclusion.

149. The last time Tristram addressed her directly in his *Life*: "I will not argue the matter: Time wastes too fast: every letter I trace tells me with what rapidity Life follows my pen; the days and hours of it, more precious, my dear Jenny! than the rubies about thy neck, are flying over our heads like light clouds of a windy day, never to return more — every thing presses on — whilst thou art twisting that lock, — see! it grows grey; and every time I kiss thy hand to bid adieu, and every absence which follows it, are preludes to

_____. — "

150. She liked to think he was somewhere in the trees.

151. By the time the bicycle was completely reconstructed, from various parts found here and there (a horn from the lady in white, who also offered spring water with healing powers; a spare tire from a junk yard in Venice; a chain from a man in the subway station; a seat from the hermit met in the library; handle bars from the old seaman; etc.), the original bike, its chrome shiny and sparkling in the moonlight, showed up on the front doorstep, somehow, overnight; however, when the protagonist spied it, she no longer wanted it, saying she preferred the one she had constructed.

152. Of course we are unfinished.

153. 62° 17′ 20″, 19° 2′ 40″ and 37.29 N, 79.52 W respectively.

154. "I felt in his pockets, one after another. A few small coins, a thimble, and some thread and big needles, a piece of pigtail tobacco bitten away at the end, his gully with the crooked handle, a pocket compass, and a tinder box were all that they contained, and I began to despair."

155. Often, she heard her father whistling, beckoning her home, and she would run, abandoning whatever game she had been playing in a neighbor's house or yard somewhere. When she returned home, her father would be calmly sitting, wanting nothing in particular, saying he had not whistled, that she must have heard this out of some sort of homesickness.

156. The essence behind the curtain, i.e. the stage, is composed of the yearning to determine what may be seen and what will remain unseen. This should be understood in the definition of "staging."

156¾. The reason why she chose green for the final act may be given in this passage from her dream log:

> . . . I was in bed with [illegible]. We were in the old house, in the room with the red carpet. We were afraid because there were people outside who wished to shoot us. I turned and asked him, "From where do you think they'll start shooting? I'm so afraid." We went out to the living area. There were others there. Outside, a girl dressed in black was by the sliding glass doors, writing in her memo book. "Close the curtains!" I heard someone say. I heard someone say no, that they were afraid. The curtains were the same green curtains from my childhood, and so I moved forth to close them because I, more than anyone, would know just how to do so. But I backed off when I thought of the possibility of being killed . . .

156.999 . . . *Translator's Note.*—This sentence in the original is obviously meant to illustrate the fault of which it speaks. It does so by the use of a construction very common in the original,[‡] but happily unknown in translation[∞]; however, the fault itself still exists nonetheless, though in different form.

[‡] *original* as in *this life.*
[∞] *translation* as in *the next.*

SHE FOLDED HER BED SHEET LIKE A LOVE LETTER, WROTE:

*If this came to you by post, then you should know how we must mar
things to prove that they exist, as I have had to do in order to be sure that
I exist; hence the postmark; hence the* used *stamp.*

SHE SHOULD RATHER NOT HAVE SENT THIS AT ALL; SHE SHOULD RATHER
THAT THE WORLD REMAINED EXTREMELY *LIFE-LIKE*. TAKE, FOR IN-
STANCE, THE PERIOD OF THE EAVESDROPPING LEAVES: WHILE THERE,
SHE KNEW IT WAS ENDING; THEREFORE, SHE BEGAN CONSRUCTING
HER STORY—CROSSING THE STREET, SHE WOULD THINK, *& THEN SHE
CROSSED THE STREET . . .*

A CERTAIN PASSAGE BY HOMER, WRITTEN ON A BOOKSHELF BY A BED
BY A SEA, WHICH BEGAN VAGUELY IN THE MANNER OF "MOUNT MY BED
WITH LOVE . . ." OR SOMETHING OR OTHER: SHE ALWAYS MEANT TO,
BUT ALWAYS FORGOT TO COPY IT.

REPLACE HER KISS WITH AN UMBRELLA; REMEMBER WHAT WAS SAID
UNDER THE SCAFFOLDING, THE SORRY SUBTEXT OF ALL OF THAT.

SHORTLY AFTERWARDS, TRISTRAM TURNED OVER HER FINAL LETTER:

*I suppose we were merely on loan in each other's lives; these last years
have already broken their secrets, have already gone out ahead and be-*

yond us, reaching their conclusions: the present was beautiful in my not knowing. There are some sufferings as crimson and fallen, vibrant as autumn's tremblings.

YET STILL, SHE DREAMT OF SENDING LETTERS, DREAMT IN THE MANNER OF MANDELSTAM:

[At a critical moment, a seafarer tosses a sealed bottle into the ocean waves, containing his name and a message detailing his fate. Wandering along the dunes many years later, I happen upon it in the sand. I read the message, not the date, the last will and testament of one who has passed on. I have the right to do so. I have not opened someone else's mail. The message in the bottle was addressed to its finder. I found it. That means, I have become its secret addressee.]

THE PARAPHRASE WOULD ALWAYS BE BAD, HER ANTENNAE BENT AND REMORSEFUL:

"I admire you, beloved, for the trap you've set": laying down all of that FALSE EVIDENCE: the rose was fake until I touched it; I warned you —do not say love, I will think Love; & I went on, following the wrong leads—the [illegible], the many possible paths, the passages you would only later delete. When it comes to pass, like this, this late, all, all transpires without asking my permission or requesting my fingerprints. & I do not know what forgets, but its letters are handed badly & I go on, existing among its belongings. It is always easy to spy the EMERGENCY EXIT, & this makes me want to save lives like a superhero. In all of the early mornings of this life, I must spit in keyholes like Frank O'Hara, & what's more: I steal other people's mail that today has not come for anybody anyhow.

AND TO THINK HOW THE LEAVES USED TO ADDRESS HER: HOW SHE SO BELIEVED SHE ALONE WAS MEANT TO DISCERN THE SIGNS AND OMENS, THE SECRET ADDRESSEE:

All night, it came again, even had the courage to sit in my rocking chair, borrowed books from my shelf, broke a teacup, took to calling me by name. I only disclose this information because, whenever the trees' branches extended their hands to me, I used to be so certain it was you, beckoning.

As ever, there was no will found among the remains.

Original version of the last sentence in the penultimate paragraph:

Let those strikes of lightning come so we will quickly know what leaves us.

—Eds.

Essay Press is dedicated to publishing innovative, explorative, and culturally relevant essays in book form. We welcome your support through the purchase of our books and through donations directly to the press. Please contact us to be added to our mailing list.

EDITORS

Eula Biss, Stephen Cope, and Catherine Taylor

ESSAY PRESS

131 North Congress Street, Athens, Ohio 45701 www.essaypress.org

New and forthcoming titles from Essay Press:

JOSHUA CASTEEL *Letters from Abu Ghraib*
ALBERT GOLDBARTH *Griffin* .
CARLA HARRYMAN *Adorno's Noise*
KRISTIN PREVALLET *I, Afterlife: Essay in Mourning Time*